# Practical Ways of Starting A Successful Business

# Practical Ways of Starting A Successful Business

Aaron Robinson
Tocarra Robinson

Robinson Publishing, LLC
Contact: (312) 715-7884

Robinson Publishing, LLC
Published by Robinson Publishing, LLC


Copyright ©2023 by Robinson Publishing, LLC

Cover Photos and Design by Robinson Publishing, LLC
Art Direction by Aaron Robinson
Edited by Robinson Publishing, LLC


ISBN: 9798861230575

I would like to give all Honor and Glory to The Most High for allowing me to be able to participate in this great experience and grow as a person. I would also like to thank my Ancestors for enduring all of their struggles and sacrifices so that I might have the opportunity and life that they were not able to enjoy. I want to thank my wife and family for being my constant motivation to constantly strive for success. I want to thank my family for never giving up on me and keeping me grounded in life. Also, I want to thank all of my mentors who I learned from that gave me the confidence to look within myself and see the potential I have and the greatness that lies within. Last but not least, I want to thank my friends and business partners for pushing me to my limits and not accepting failure or excuses on our journey to success!

Aaron Robinson


There are numerous people I would like to thank for their unconditional support throughout my life. Without your support I would not be the successful person I am today. For that, I am extremely grateful and would like to acknowledge and thank those who have played a vital role and had the greatest impact in my life. First, I would like to thank my nurturing and caring husband, Aaron Robinson; without your support, many of my endeavors, including this book would not have been possible. I would like to extend my sincere thanks to my mother, Lavern Eldridge, who is inspirational to me and sticks with me through all life's challenges. I'd also like to thank everyone else who has played an instrumental role along my journey.

Tocarra Eldridge Robinson

# TABLE OF CONTENTS

# INTRODUCTION

Welcome to the world of entrepreneurship, where ideas come to life, and dreams transform into reality. This Book is your compass, guiding you through the exhilarating journey of starting and nurturing a successful business. Whether you're driven by a passion to share your unique skills, eager to introduce an innovative product, or ready to serve a niche market with your exceptional services, this guide is here to light your path.

Have you ever felt that burning desire to create something of your own? Perhaps you've envisioned a solution to a problem or have a talent you're eager to turn into a profession. The purpose of starting a business varies from person to person – financial independence, creative fulfillment, making a difference in your community, or a blend of these aspirations. As we embark on this journey together, we'll explore the myriad reasons that fuel the entrepreneur's spirit.

Imagine having a trusted companion by your side, sharing insights garnered from their own business adventures. In the vast landscape of entrepreneurship, seeking guidance is like finding a treasure map. Mentors who've walked the path before can provide invaluable advice, helping you avoid pitfalls and embrace opportunities. Discover the power of resources like business centers, associations, and SCORE mentors – your allies in shaping your business vision.

Are you drawn to offering a service that resonates with your expertise, or perhaps you're eager to craft a product that will leave a mark? The decision is yours, but it's important to know the lay of the land. Delve into the considerations of startup costs, whether you'll bootstrap, seek investors, or secure a loan. Your journey begins with this decision, laying the foundation for the business you're about to birth.

Names have a magical ability to capture the essence of things. Think about it – the moment you hear certain brand names, your mind conjures images and feelings. Your business name should be no different. It's your first impression, your calling card. Alongside, imagine a logo that's more than just an image; it's a symbol that encapsulates your brand's personality. The process of naming and designing isn't just about aesthetics; it's about creating a magnetic identity that draws customers to you.

Every business venture is a legal entity, subject to a set of regulations and requirements. It might sound daunting, but it's the sturdy framework that ensures your business operates ethically and seamlessly. Don't worry; we'll break it down step by step. From filing the right documents to obtaining essential identifications, we're here to demystify the legal landscape and empower you to navigate it confidently.

A business without a plan is like a ship without a course. This blueprint isn't just for investors – it's your guiding star. In this section, we'll delve into creating a compelling mission, setting achievable goals, and understanding your target audience. This plan isn't static; it's your dynamic roadmap to steer your business toward growth and prosperity.

Now that your business has taken shape, it's time for the world to know. Marketing isn't just about advertisements; it's about telling your story. From business cards to websites, from social media to word of mouth, we'll explore avenues that give your business the attention it deserves. Together, we'll craft strategies that resonate, connecting you with your audience in meaningful ways.

Business isn't just about products and services; it's about connections. Networking is the thread that weaves your business into the fabric of the industry. As you attend events, join associations, and mingle with fellow entrepreneurs, you're building bridges that can sustain your business through collaborations, partnerships, and shared wisdom. We'll explore the art of networking and unveil the treasure trove of resources available to you.

With this Book as your guide, you're equipped to embark on a transformative journey. The path of entrepreneurship is exhilarating and sometimes challenging, but it's a voyage worth taking. As we navigate through each chapter, remember that you're not alone; you have a wealth of knowledge and support at your fingertips. So, let's dive in and unravel the practical ways of starting a successful business. Your adventure begins now.

# CHAPTER 1:
# THE PURPOSE OF STARTING A BUSINESS

At the heart of every successful business lies a driving purpose – a reason that propels individuals to take the plunge into entrepreneurship. Understanding your purpose is the foundation upon which you'll build your business and shape its trajectory. In this chapter, we will explore the myriad motivations that inspire people to start their own ventures and how these motivations align with various business paths. By delving into the essence of why you're embarking on this journey, you'll gain a clearer understanding of the direction you want your business to take.

## Unveiling Motivations:

The decision to embark on the entrepreneurial journey is often spurred by a complex web of motivations, dreams, and desires. These motivations serve as the emotional underpinning that propels you forward, even in the face of challenges.

The motivations driving individuals to start a business are as diverse as the entrepreneurs themselves. Let's take a closer look at some of the most common motivations that drive individuals to start their own businesses:

1. Freedom and Independence: The desire for autonomy and control over one's work and schedule.
2. Pursuit of Passion: Transforming a hobby or skill into a business, driven by genuine enthusiasm.
3. Financial Prosperity: Seeking the potential for substantial earnings and financial security.
4. Creating Impact: Using business as a means to make a positive difference in society or the environment.

5.  Work-Life Balance: Striving to achieve equilibrium between work and personal life.
6.  Challenging the Status Quo: Motivated by disrupting norms and introducing innovative solutions.
7.  Legacy and Longevity: Building a lasting legacy and leaving a mark on the industry.
8.  Personal Growth: Viewing entrepreneurship as a path for continuous learning and self-improvement.
9.  Autonomy and Creativity: Harnessing the opportunity to express creativity across all aspects of the business.
10. Filling a Gap: Identifying market voids and providing solutions that others overlook.
11. Overcoming Challenges: Driven by the satisfaction of conquering obstacles and turning adversity into opportunity.

These motivations not only shape the direction of businesses but also define the entrepreneur's journey. Recognizing and embracing these driving forces is essential, as they become the foundation upon which successful businesses are built. Your motivations will guide decisions, inspire innovation, and fuel your determination, ensuring that your journey in entrepreneurship remains purposeful and fulfilling.

## Charting Your Business Path

Once you've uncovered your motivations, it's time to align them with a specific business path. If you're considering a service-based business, think about how your skills, knowledge, and expertise can be transformed into valuable offerings. If product creation excites you, envision how your innovation can address a gap in the market. This alignment ensures that your business venture becomes a seamless extension of your passions and abilities. Let's delve deeper into how you can navigate this crucial step and choose a business path that resonates with your unique strengths:

1. Leverage Expertise: Your skills and expertise are valuable assets that can be transformed into a service-based business. Consider how you can offer solutions based on what you're proficient in.

2. Embrace Passion: Your passions can be the driving force behind your business. Transforming a beloved hobby into a business not only fuels your enthusiasm but also provides an authentic foundation.

3. Product Innovation: If you have a unique product that fulfills a market need, a product-based business might be your path. Ensure your product offers value and meets customer demands.

4. Problem Solving: Successful businesses address real problems. Identify challenges and create solutions that resonate with your audience to position yourself as a valuable solution provider.

5. Personal Branding: Building a business around your personal brand is a strategy that capitalizes on your unique perspective, knowledge, or story.

6. Stay Trend-Ready: Pay attention to market trends to spot emerging opportunities. Trends like sustainability and technological advancements can inspire innovative business ideas.

7. Local vs. Global: Decide whether your business will cater to a local community, a national audience, or a global market, aligning your business model with your intended reach.

8. Franchise or Independent: Choose between starting an independent venture or exploring franchise opportunities, considering factors like creative freedom and established business models.
9. Value Proposition: Articulate what sets your business apart and how your offerings benefit customers. A strong value proposition guides marketing efforts and resonates with your target audience.
10. Long-Term Vision: Align your business path with your long-term vision – whether it's a side hustle, a full-time endeavor, or a scalable enterprise.

Selecting your business path is the compass that will guide your entrepreneurial journey. By aligning it with your core motivations, you're setting the stage for a venture that reflects your values, passions, and aspirations. Your chosen path becomes the conduit through which you turn dreams into tangible success.

## Balancing Passion and Profit

The equilibrium between passion and profit is the heartbeat of a successful business. Passion infuses your venture with authenticity, driving your commitment and attracting like-minded customers. However, profit is the practical backbone that ensures your business's sustainability and growth.

Passion is the force that propels you forward, permeating every aspect of your business. It's the enthusiasm that captivates customers and makes your offerings stand out. Yet, profit is the financial foundation that transforms your passion into a viable enterprise. It enables you to invest in expansion, refine your products, and withstand economic fluctuations.

The art lies in setting prices that reflect both the value you offer and the costs of delivering that value. Passion aligns with profit when you identify where your offerings meet market demand. This convergence not only brings financial rewards but deepens your connection to your business's purpose.

Sustainability hinges on striking a harmonious balance. Reinvesting profits fuels growth, allowing your business to make a more significant impact. Regular assessments of strategies, financial statements, and cost-efficiency keep your passion-driven venture on track.

In essence, harmonizing passion and profit creates a virtuous cycle. Passion fuels your dedication, and profit empowers you to amplify that dedication. Balancing these forces ensures your business thrives emotionally, ethically, and financially, leading to enduring success.

## Evaluating Market Fit

Evaluating market fit is the process of aligning your business's purpose with the needs of your target audience. To achieve this, understanding your audience is paramount. Segment your customers based on demographics, behaviors, and preferences. Pinpoint their pain points – the challenges they face that your business can address. Keep an eye on market trends and technological advancements, adapting your purpose to stay relevant.

Competitor analysis provides insights into existing gaps in the market while validating your concept with potential customers ensures that your offerings resonate. Crafting a unique value proposition (UVP) encapsulates why your business is the solution it needs.

Ultimately, the market fit is the intersection of your passion and the needs of your audience. It's a dynamic process that requires ongoing assessment and adjustment to ensure your business's viability and success.

## Embracing Flexibility

While your purpose serves as your North Star, don't forget that the entrepreneurial journey is marked by unexpected twists. Your purpose might remain constant, but the strategies to achieve it can evolve. Be open to adapting your business model based on customer feedback, market trends, and technological advancements. Flexibility allows your purpose to guide you while also enabling you to capitalize on new opportunities.

In the world of entrepreneurship, flexibility isn't just a strategy, but a mindset that can shape the trajectory of your business journey. It's the art of adapting without compromising your purpose, allowing you to navigate challenges, seize opportunities, and evolve gracefully. Embracing flexibility involves:

1. Responding to Feedback: Utilize feedback to refine your strategies and enhance your offerings while staying aligned with your purpose.
2. Pivoting with Purpose: Adjust your direction strategically to align with market demands, ensuring your purpose remains steadfast even as paths shift.

3. Seizing Emerging Opportunities: Recognize and leverage unexpected opportunities that align with your purpose, enhancing your business's growth potential.
4. Navigating Challenges: View challenges as learning experiences, using flexibility to maneuver through obstacles while staying committed to your purpose.
5. Balancing Vision and Adaptation: Strike a harmonious balance between your unwavering purpose and the necessary adaptations required to thrive in a dynamic environment.
6. The Evolution of Your Purpose: Understand that your purpose can evolve over time, and flexibility allows you to adjust your strategies to accommodate these changes.

Embracing flexibility doesn't dilute your purpose; rather, it amplifies it by ensuring your journey remains aligned with your core values. As you navigate the entrepreneurial landscape, remember that while your purpose serves as your guiding star, flexibility equips you with the tools to navigate uncharted waters with confidence and poise.

In the tapestry of entrepreneurship, your purpose is the thread that weaves together your dreams, goals, and actions. Understanding the underlying motivations behind starting a business gives your journey a strong foundation. By aligning your passions with market needs, you craft a business that resonates deeply with both you and your customers. Embrace your purpose, but remain adaptable in your approach. As you move forward, remember that your purpose will be the driving force that keeps you focused and motivated, even when faced with challenges.

Your journey in entrepreneurship has begun, and with a clear sense of purpose, you're equipped for success.

# CHAPTER 2:
# SEEKING GUIDANCE AND COUNSELING

In the intricate realm of entrepreneurship, seeking guidance and counseling is akin to acquiring a treasure map that leads you through uncharted territories. This chapter is your compass, directing you to mentors, resources, and insights that can steer your business toward success. By harnessing the wisdom of those who've walked the path before you and tapping into invaluable resources, you'll set the stage for informed decision-making and confident strides in your entrepreneurial journey.

## The Power of Mentorship

Mentorship in the realm of entrepreneurship is a beacon of guidance, offering seasoned insights and practical wisdom to those embarking on their business journey. Much more than mere advice, a mentor acts as a personal GPS, guiding entrepreneurs through challenges and opportunities with the benefit of their experiences. Their real-world lessons provide a roadmap, enabling mentees to make informed decisions and sidestep pitfalls.

Mentors tailor their advice to the unique needs of each mentee, offering customized solutions that address specific business scenarios. Their networks of connections and resources serve as invaluable assets, opening doors to collaborations and partnerships. Mentorship instills confidence in decision-making, providing a supportive sounding board for choices that define a business's trajectory.

Beyond practical guidance, mentors offer encouragement and resilience during the highs and lows of entrepreneurship. Their belief in a mentee's potential becomes a wellspring of inspiration. Mentorship isn't just a transaction – it's a transformative relationship that shapes character and mindset. As mentees inherit the legacy of knowledge, they, in turn, contribute to the cycle by mentoring others, and creating a community of growth and wisdom.

In the world of business, mentorship is the torch that lights the way, allowing aspiring entrepreneurs to navigate the path with confidence, inspired by the footsteps of those who've gone before. Embracing mentorship is a gift that not only accelerates success but also contributes to a legacy of shared wisdom across generations.

## Navigating Business Centers

Business centers are vibrant hubs of knowledge and support, offering essential resources to guide aspiring entrepreneurs on their journey. These centers provide access to expert guidance through mentors and professionals who share practical insights and advice. Tailored workshops and training sessions equip entrepreneurs with vital skills, while networking opportunities connect them with potential partners and collaborators.

Business centers foster a supportive community, allowing entrepreneurs to share their experiences, successes, and challenges. These centers also keep entrepreneurs updated on industry trends, ensuring they remain adaptable and relevant in the ever-changing business landscape. By actively engaging with business centers, entrepreneurs can tap into a wealth of resources, connections, and knowledge that empower them to navigate the complexities of entrepreneurship and achieve their goals.

## Leveraging Small Business Associations

Small Business Associations (SBAs) stand as valuable resources for entrepreneurs, offering a range of advantages that can significantly impact your business journey. These associations provide networking opportunities through workshops, conferences, and industry events, allowing you to connect with peers, industry experts, and potential clients. Mentorship within SBAs offers guidance from experienced professionals who have navigated the challenges of entrepreneurship, helping you make informed decisions and accelerate your learning curve.

Educational resources within SBAs empower you with essential skills and knowledge, from business planning to marketing strategies. SBAs also advocate for small businesses, representing your interests in policy-making and ensuring a conducive business environment. Access to funding and financial assistance programs can fuel your business growth, particularly in its early stages.

Tailored industry insights keep you informed about market trends, regulations, and advancements specific to your field. The sense of community found within SBAs provides a supportive space for collaboration, camaraderie, and idea exchange among like-minded entrepreneurs.

By leveraging SBAs, you tap into an ecosystem that nurtures your business's growth and enhances your professional journey. The connections, mentorship, education, and resources offered by SBAs are invaluable assets that can propel you toward achieving your business goals.

## Unveiling SCORE

In the intricate world of entrepreneurship, SCORE shines as a beacon of support and wisdom. The Service Corps of Retired Executives (SCORE), a nonprofit organization, offers a haven for both new and experienced entrepreneurs. With a vast network of over 10,000 volunteer mentors, SCORE provides personalized guidance that can profoundly influence your business journey.

The core of SCORE's magic lies in the mentor-mentee connection. These seasoned mentors, with their diverse backgrounds and wealth of experience, offer tailor-made advice for every stage of your entrepreneurial venture. Whether you're crafting a business idea or facing growth challenges, SCORE mentors stand ready with insights that can transform obstacles into opportunities.

Beyond one-on-one mentoring, SCORE enriches your learning through workshops, webinars, and online resources. These educational offerings cover an array of business facets, from marketing strategies to financial management. By tapping into these resources, you arm yourself with knowledge that empowers you to tackle various entrepreneurial tasks.

SCORE instills confidence in entrepreneurs, helping them navigate the complex terrain of business ownership. The organization's accessibility, whether through in-person meetings or virtual connections, ensures that anyone, regardless of location, can tap into their wisdom.

In essence, SCORE isn't just an organization – it's a catalyst for your business's success. By harnessing the guidance of seasoned mentors, accessing educational resources, and becoming part of a supportive network, you position yourself for entrepreneurial triumph. With SCORE by your side, you're not just embarking on a business journey; you're embarking on a journey of growth, empowerment, and meaningful achievement.

## Setting Clear Goals

Setting clear goals is the compass that guides your business journey, translating your aspirations into achievable milestones. By adhering to the SMART framework – Specific, Measurable, Achievable, Relevant, and Time-bound – you transform vague intentions into well-defined targets. Breaking down long-term goals into manageable steps creates checkpoints for tracking progress and maintaining motivation.

Aligning goals with your mission ensures that each achievement contributes to your business's overarching purpose. Regular evaluation and adjustment allow you to adapt to changing circumstances and market dynamics. Goals provide both intrinsic motivation and external accountability, propelling you forward with a sense of purpose.

Visualization and celebrating milestones bolster your determination. Ultimately, clear goals are the threads that weave your business's success story, guiding you from envisioning possibilities to realizing accomplishments. Embrace this transformative mindset as you navigate the challenges and triumphs of entrepreneurship, always keeping your North Star – your mission – in sight.

## Building a Support Network

Establishing a robust support network is a vital pillar of success. This network consists of mentors, peers, business centers, associations, online communities, and networking events. Mentors bring wisdom and guidance, peers offer camaraderie and collaboration, and associations provide knowledge hubs. Online communities transcend geographic boundaries, while networking events sow the seeds of opportunity.

Investing in relationships is a two-way street, where reciprocity and value exchange strengthen bonds. This network isn't just about seeking advice; it's about continuous learning, broadening perspectives, and inspiring innovation. Your support network becomes the bedrock that empowers you to navigate challenges, celebrate victories, and sustain your entrepreneurial journey.

As you waltz through the dance of entrepreneurship, remember that you're not alone – you have a chorus of support that harmonizes with your aspirations, offering guidance, encouragement, and a shared vision of success.

Seeking guidance and counseling is not a sign of weakness, but a testament to your commitment to success. By tapping into the wisdom of mentors, business centers, associations, and resources like SCORE, you're arming yourself with knowledge that can guide your decisions and actions. Remember that every successful entrepreneur has leaned on the advice of others at some point in their journey. As you embark on this path, keep an open mind, absorb insights, and let the guidance you receive shape your business's trajectory. With the right mentors and resources by your side, you're equipped to navigate the challenges and opportunities of entrepreneurship with confidence.

# CHAPTER 3:
## DECIDING ON
## SERVICES PROVIDED

The heart of your business lies in the services you offer – the solutions you bring to the table, the expertise you share, and the value you provide to your customers. This chapter delves into the critical process of deciding on the services you'll offer, understanding your target market, and carefully evaluating the financial aspects that will shape your business's foundation.

## Defining Your Service Portfolio

Your journey begins by defining the scope of your services. Are you offering consulting, design, writing, or perhaps a combination of specialized skills? The key is to align your offerings with your strengths and passions. This section will guide you through assessing your expertise and identifying the services that not only resonate with you but also address market needs.

Your service portfolio is the foundation upon which your business stands, the suite of solutions you offer to address the needs of your target audience. It's not just a list of services; it's a reflection of your expertise, passion, and the unique value you bring to the market. To define your service portfolio effectively, consider these key steps:

1. Assess Your Expertise: Take an inventory of your skills, knowledge, and experience. What are you exceptionally good at? What solutions can you provide that others can't? Your service portfolio should align with your strengths and expertise.
2. Address Market Needs: Identify gaps in the market that your services can fill. Look for pain points that your target audience is experiencing but haven't been adequately addressed. Crafting services that directly address these needs positions you as a problem solver.

3. Niche vs. Broad Services: Decide whether you want to offer a broad range of services or specialize in a specific niche. Specialization can make you a go-to expert in a particular area, while offering a broader range of services can attract a wider audience.
4. Align with Your Brand: Your service portfolio should align seamlessly with your brand's identity and values. It should convey what your business stands for and create a consistent experience for your customers.
5. Evolvability: Consider the scalability and adaptability of your service offerings. As your business grows, can your services evolve to cater to changing customer needs and market trends?

## Understanding Your Target Market

Every successful business understands its customers intimately. Identify your target market – the individuals or businesses that will benefit the most from your services. Consider demographics, pain points, and preferences. By understanding your audience, you can tailor your services to meet their specific needs, giving your business a competitive edge.

Your target market is the group of individuals or businesses that are most likely to benefit from your services. Understanding them intimately is essential for tailoring your offerings to their needs. Here's how to gain a deeper understanding of your target market:

1. Demographics and Psychographics: Start by defining the demographics – age, gender, location, income – of your potential customers. Then, dive into their psychographics – their interests, values, preferences, and behaviors.

2. Pain Points and Needs: What challenges do your target customers face? What problems do they need solutions for? Identifying their pain points allows you to craft services that directly address their concerns.
3. Behavioral Insights: Understand how your target audience interacts with products and services similar to yours. What are their buying behaviors? Where do they look for information? This insight informs your marketing strategies.
4. Segmentation: Depending on the diversity of your audience, consider segmenting it into smaller groups with similar characteristics. This allows you to tailor your services and messaging more effectively.

## Analyzing Market Demand

Market demand is the driving force behind your business's success. Research and analyze the demand for the services you plan to offer. Is there a gap that you can fill? Is there a unique approach you can bring to the table? This section will guide you in assessing the market landscape, ensuring that your services align with existing needs and trends.

Here's how to assess market demand:

1. Research Existing Solutions: Investigate the competition. Are there similar services in the market? What do they offer? Identifying gaps or areas for improvement can lead to innovative service ideas.
2. Conduct Surveys and Interviews: Engage directly with potential customers through surveys or interviews. Ask about their needs, pain points, and

willingness to pay for solutions. This primary research provides invaluable insights.

3. Trends and Industry Reports: Stay updated with industry trends and reports. Are there emerging needs or shifts in consumer preferences? Adapting to these trends can give you a competitive edge.
4. Test the Waters: Consider offering a limited version of your services or a pilot program to gauge interest and demand. This can help you refine your offerings before a full launch.
5. Forecasting: Use collected data to create demand forecasts. Project how the demand for your services might evolve over time, helping you plan for growth and resource allocation.

Understanding market demand ensures that your services are not only relevant but also in high demand. By thoroughly analyzing the needs of your target audience and the landscape of existing solutions, you position your business for success in a market that craves what you offer.

## Calculating Startup Costs

Estimating startup costs is a pivotal exercise that lays the foundation for your business's financial planning. Beyond your core idea and enthusiasm, practical realities like funding requirements and initial investments come into play. Startup costs encompass a range of expenses, including tangible assets like equipment, inventory, and facilities, as well as intangibles like branding and marketing.

Begin by identifying your essential assets. What equipment, tools, or technology do you need to kick-start your operations? Consider both one-time purchases and ongoing operational expenses, such as rent, utilities, and employee salaries. Don't forget to account for licenses, permits, and legal fees necessary to establish your business's legitimacy.

In addition to the basics, factor in potential unexpected costs. A buffer for contingencies ensures that you're prepared to tackle unforeseen challenges that might arise during your business's early stages.

Remember, while conservative estimates are prudent, avoid underestimating your costs. A thorough understanding of your financial requirements allows you to secure adequate funding and ensures that you're well-prepared for the initial phases of your business journey.

## Exploring Funding Options

Startup capital is the fuel that propels your business forward. As you embark on your entrepreneurial journey, you'll need to assess your funding options to ensure you have the necessary resources to bring your business to life. Consider a spectrum of funding avenues:

1. Self-Funding: Using personal savings or assets to finance your venture. While it offers autonomy, it can be limited by your personal financial situation.
2. Friends and Family: Seeking investment from close connections who believe in your vision. Maintain transparency and clearly outline terms to avoid strained relationships.
3. Angel Investors: High-net-worth individuals who provide capital in exchange for equity. Their expertise and network can be invaluable assets.

4. Venture Capital: Venture capitalists invest in startups with high growth potential in exchange for equity. This avenue is suitable for businesses aiming for rapid expansion.
5. Crowdfunding: Raising funds from a large number of individuals through platforms like Kickstarter or Indiegogo. Effective storytelling and compelling rewards are crucial here.
6. Bank Loans: Traditional bank loans provide funding, but require a solid credit history and collateral. Be prepared to manage interest payments.
7. Small Business Grants: Government agencies and private organizations offer grants to support specific business endeavors. Research eligibility criteria and application processes.
8. Incubators and Accelerators: These programs provide funding, mentorship, and resources in exchange for equity. They often focus on early-stage startups.

Each funding option comes with its pros and cons. Assess your business's needs, growth trajectory, and comfort level with relinquishing equity or taking on debt. A well-thought-out funding strategy aligns your financial needs with your business's aspirations.

## Balancing Investment and Return

Investment is the lifeblood of your business, and achieving a balance between your investments and expected returns is crucial. Determining how much to invest in various aspects of your business requires careful consideration.

First, understand the nature of your business and its industry. Some businesses demand higher upfront investments due to the need for equipment, inventory, or skilled labor. In contrast, others might operate with lower initial costs but require ongoing investments in marketing or research and development.

Consider the timelines for return on investment (ROI). Some investments yield immediate returns, while others might take months or even years to materialize. Align your investment expectations with the pace at which your business generates revenue.

Moreover, evaluate the risk-reward ratio. While it's important to invest in growth, overextending your resources can lead to financial strain. Maintaining a prudent balance ensures that you're positioning your business for sustainable growth without compromising its financial stability.

## Building a Financial Projection

A financial projection is the compass that guides your business's financial decisions. It's a forecast of your anticipated income, expenses, and profits over a specified period. Building a comprehensive financial projection involves a blend of informed estimations and data analysis. Start by outlining your revenue streams. How much can you reasonably expect to earn from your products or services? Consider different pricing scenarios and sales projections based on market research.

Next, delve into your expenses. Categorize them into fixed (e.g., rent, utilities) and variable (e.g., raw materials, marketing). Be meticulous in estimating costs, as accuracy is key to a reliable projection.

Consider your cash flow – the timing of when money comes in and goes out. This helps you anticipate periods of surplus and potential shortfalls. A positive cash flow is vital for maintaining your business's day-to-day operations and growth initiatives.

Assemble your projection into a clear format, showcasing monthly or quarterly figures. Use financial software or spreadsheets to calculate totals, percentages, and margins. Sensitivity analysis, where you evaluate the impact of various factors on your projections, is also beneficial to understand potential risks.

Remember that projections aren't set in stone – they're a dynamic tool that requires regular review and adjustment based on real-world performance. As your business progresses, update your projections to reflect actual outcomes. A well-constructed financial projection is a valuable decision-making tool that empowers you to make informed choices, secure funding, and stay on course toward achieving your business's financial objectives.

Deciding on the services you'll offer forms the bedrock of your business. Through careful analysis of your expertise, market demand, and financial considerations, you'll create a service portfolio that resonates with your target audience. By aligning your offerings with market needs and calculating startup costs, you'll set the stage for a strong foundation. Remember, the services you provide are not just transactions; they're solutions that have the power to make a difference in the lives of your customers. As you embark on this journey, keep your commitment to value and excellence at the forefront of your decisions.

# CHAPTER 4:
# CREATING A BUSINESS NAME AND IDENTITY

Your business's name and identity are more than just labels – they are the face of your brand, the first impression you make on your customers, and the foundation of your business's personality. This chapter explores the art of crafting a memorable business name, designing a captivating logo, and building an identity that resonates with your target audience.

## Choosing the Perfect Business Name

Selecting the ideal name for your business is a pivotal step that resonates far beyond a mere label. Your business name is a gateway to your brand's identity and essence. It's the first impression you make on potential customers, partners, and investors. A well-chosen name can embody your values, convey your mission, and spark curiosity.

Brainstorming is a creative journey – a process where you explore words, concepts, and combinations that reflect your business's spirit. Consider elements that encapsulate your unique offerings, evoke positive emotions, and have the potential to be memorable. Your name should be a fusion of relevance and originality, aligning with your vision and standing out in a crowded marketplace.

Remember, your business name will be with you for the long haul. It will grace your website, signage, marketing materials, and conversations. Visualize your business's future as you brainstorm, imagining how your chosen name will resonate with customers and become synonymous with your brand's success.

## The Power of Visuals: Designing Your Logo

A logo is the visual embodiment of your brand's identity. It's a powerful tool that transcends language, communicating your business's essence at a single glance. Your logo carries the responsibility of encapsulating your values, showcasing your professionalism, and leaving a lasting impression.

Effective logo design is a blend of art and strategy. Colors evoke emotions, and typography conveys personality. The right combination of shapes and imagery can convey sophistication, playfulness, or innovation. Each element is meticulously chosen to align with your brand's message and resonate with your target audience.

Crafting a logo involves envisioning it across various mediums – from business cards to digital platforms. A versatile logo adapts to different contexts while maintaining its impact and recognition. As you embark on logo design, remember that your logo is a bridge between your business's visual identity and the emotions it evokes in your customers.

## Crafting a Memorable Tagline

A tagline is the distilled essence of your brand's promise. It's a concise statement that encapsulates your mission, values, and unique value proposition. Crafting a memorable tagline is like composing poetry – every word matters, and brevity packs a punch.

A compelling tagline captures attention and sparks curiosity, inviting people to learn more about your business. It's a verbal snapshot of your brand's personality, tone, and offerings. The best taglines are simple yet impactful, conveying a sense of clarity while igniting intrigue.

To create a memorable tagline, start by identifying what sets your business apart. What is the core benefit you offer? How do you solve your customers' problems? Infuse your tagline with these answers and infuse it with the essence of your brand. A well-crafted tagline lingers in the minds of your audience, creating a mental connection between your brand and the solution it provides.

## Building a Cohesive Visual Identity

A cohesive visual identity is the harmonious marriage of your business's visual elements. From your logo and color palette to typography and design style, each component works together to create a consistent and memorable brand presence.

Think of your visual identity as a language that communicates your brand's personality. Consistency across all touchpoints – website, social media, marketing materials – fosters recognition and trust. When a customer sees your content, they should instantly recognize it as yours.

Building a cohesive visual identity involves making deliberate choices that reflect your brand's ethos. Your color palette conveys emotions, your typography sets the tone, and your design style reflects your industry and audience. Approach each visual element with purpose, knowing that they contribute to the symphony that is your brand's visual identity.

## Ensuring Brand Consistency

Brand consistency is the thread that weaves through every interaction your business has with the world. It's about creating a unified and recognizable image that reinforces your identity. Consistency extends beyond your logo and color palette – it encompasses your messaging, tone of voice, and customer experience. Every touchpoint, from your website to your social media posts, should exude the same essence.

Imagine a customer encountering your brand on different platforms – your website, social media profiles, and promotional materials. If the visual elements, messaging, and overall feel align seamlessly, it creates a sense of trust and reliability. Brand consistency not only strengthens your identity but also makes your business memorable, setting the stage for lasting customer relationships.

## The Legal Aspect: Trademarks and Copyrights

In the digital age, protecting your brand's unique identity is paramount. Trademarks and copyrights provide legal safeguards that prevent unauthorized use of your intellectual property. A trademark safeguards your brand name, logo, and tagline, ensuring that others can't use them without your permission. Copyright, on the other hand, protects original creative works, such as written content, images, and videos.

Registering trademarks and copyrights not only grants you legal ownership but also sends a clear message that your business is committed to protecting its brand identity. It prevents confusion in the market and safeguards the reputation you've worked hard to build. Consulting with legal experts in intellectual property can guide you through the process and help you navigate the legal landscape with confidence.

## Evolving Your Identity: Adapting to Growth

As your business evolves, so should your brand identity. Growth often brings new offerings, expanded target audiences, and shifting industry trends. Adapting your identity doesn't mean abandoning your core values – rather, it's about aligning your brand with your business's evolution while staying true to your essence.

Consider the iconic brands that have seamlessly evolved over time. They retained elements that made them recognizable while embracing new aesthetics that resonated with their current audience. Whether it's adjusting your logo, refreshing your website design, or revisiting your messaging, evolving your identity is a strategic move that keeps your brand relevant and compelling.

Evolving your identity requires a delicate balance. Consult with your team and gather insights from your audience. Analyze market trends and competitor strategies. Embrace change as an opportunity to refine your visual identity, revisit your messaging, and adapt to the evolving needs of your customers. By doing so, you position your business for continued growth while maintaining the trust and recognition you've earned.

Crafting a business name and identity is more than an exercise in aesthetics – it's a strategic process that shapes how your business is perceived. By choosing a compelling name, designing a captivating logo, and building a cohesive visual identity, you create a brand that resonates with your target audience. Your business's name becomes synonymous with your values, and your logo serves as a beacon that draws customers toward your offerings. As you embark on this branding journey, remember that your identity is an investment that pays off through recognition, trust, and lasting customer connections.

# CHAPTER 5:
# LEGAL STRUCTURE AND MODEL

Navigating the legal landscape is a crucial step in establishing a solid foundation for your business. This chapter delves into the various legal considerations you need to address, from selecting the right business structure to obtaining essential licenses and registrations. Understanding the legal aspects of your business ensures compliance, protection, and a smooth path forward.

## Choosing the Right Legal Structure

Selecting the appropriate legal structure for your business is a pivotal decision that affects its operations, taxation, and liability. Each structure has its own implications, so it's crucial to understand the nuances before making your choice.

- Sole Proprietorship: This simplest form of business structure involves a single owner who bears all responsibilities and liabilities. While it offers autonomy and easy setup, keep in mind that personal assets are at risk in case of business-related issues.
- Partnership: If you're teaming up with others, a partnership might be suitable. This structure divides responsibilities and profits among partners, but remember that each partner's actions can affect the others' liabilities.
- Limited Liability Company (LLC): An LLC combines flexibility and limited liability. It shields your personal assets from business debts, yet allows you to retain a level of simplicity in operations. It's a popular choice for small businesses seeking legal protection.
- Corporation: Forming a corporation provides strong liability protection, as the corporation is considered a separate entity. While it involves more complex

formalities and regulations, it can attract investors and is suitable for businesses with substantial growth aspirations.

## Understanding Liability and Protection
The legal structure you choose influences your business's liability and your personal financial security. In a sole proprietorship or partnership, your personal assets are vulnerable to business-related claims. Opting for an LLC or corporation shields your personal assets, limiting liability to the business's assets.

Limited liability means that if your business faces financial setbacks or legal issues, your personal assets like your home and savings are generally protected. This separation safeguards your financial well-being and provides peace of mind as you navigate the challenges of entrepreneurship.

## Registering Your Business
Registering your business is a critical step toward legitimizing your operations and ensuring compliance with local regulations. The specific requirements vary based on your chosen structure and your location, but generally, registering involves:
1. Business Certificate: If operating under a name other than your legal name, you'll likely need a Business Certificate or fictitious name registration.
2. Articles of Incorporation: Corporations need to file Articles of Incorporation with the state to establish their legal existence.
3. Operating Agreement: An LLC often requires an operating agreement that outlines its internal workings, such as management and distribution of profits.

4. Partnership Agreement: Partnerships can benefit from a partnership agreement that defines roles, responsibilities, and profit-sharing.

Each registration step solidifies your business's legitimacy and sets you on the path to compliance, allowing you to focus on growth and success.

## Securing an EIN and Tax Identification

An Employer Identification Number (EIN), also known as a Tax Identification Number (TIN), is like a Social Security number for your business. Even if you don't have employees, obtaining an EIN is essential for several reasons:

1. Tax Purposes: You'll need an EIN to file taxes, whether as a sole proprietor, corporation, or any other structure.
2. Business Bank Account: Most banks require an EIN to open a business bank account.
3. Legal Documentation: Applying for licenses, permits, or contracts often requires an EIN.
4. Professional Appearance: An EIN lends a professional touch to your business, signaling that you're a legitimate entity.

Obtaining an EIN is typically a straightforward process, and it's a fundamental step toward establishing your business's financial identity and complying with tax regulations.

## Navigating Industry-Specific Regulations

Industries often come with their own set of regulations and requirements that businesses must adhere to. Navigating these industry-specific regulations is vital to ensure that your business operates within legal boundaries and maintains the highest standards of compliance. Regulations can range from health and safety standards to environmental regulations and licensing requirements.

Researching and understanding these regulations is crucial before launching your business. Identify the regulatory bodies relevant to your industry and ensure that you have all the necessary permits and licenses in place. Failing to comply with industry regulations can lead to fines, legal troubles, and reputational damage. Consider consulting with experts or industry associations to stay up-to-date with evolving regulations and ensure that your business remains on the right side of the law.

## Trademarking and Intellectual Property

Your business's intellectual property – including your business name, logo, slogans, and creative content – is a valuable asset that deserves protection. Trademarking is the process of legally registering your intellectual property to prevent others from using it without your permission. It safeguards your brand identity and prevents confusion among customers.

Trademarking involves conducting thorough searches to ensure that your chosen business name or logo doesn't infringe on existing trademarks. Once registered, your trademark provides legal recourse in case of unauthorized use. Protecting your intellectual property early on prevents legal battles down the road and maintains the integrity of your brand.

Additionally, consider copyrighting your original creative works, such as written content, artwork, and music, to further safeguard your intellectual property rights.

Consulting with legal professionals specializing in intellectual property can provide invaluable guidance in navigating this complex realm.

## Obtaining a DUNS Number

A Data Universal Numbering System (DUNS) number is a unique nine-digit identifier assigned to businesses by Dun & Bradstreet. It's often required for business transactions, particularly if you plan to work with government agencies or larger corporations. A DUNS number helps these entities assess the creditworthiness and reliability of your business.

Obtaining a DUNS number is a straightforward process. You can apply for one through the Dun & Bradstreet website. This number not only enhances your business's credibility but also opens doors to opportunities that require this unique identifier. Having a DUNS number is especially beneficial if you're looking to establish partnerships, bid for government contracts, or access certain funding options.

## Legal Counsel and Consultation

Navigating legal matters can be intricate and overwhelming. Seeking legal counsel and consultation is a prudent step to ensure that your business operates within legal boundaries and avoids potential pitfalls. Legal professionals specializing in business law can provide valuable insights and expertise tailored to your specific industry and location.

From drafting contracts and agreements to understanding complex regulations, legal experts can guide you through various legal processes. Their assistance can help you avoid costly mistakes, ensure compliance, and protect your business's interests. Establishing a relationship with a trusted legal advisor offers peace of mind, allowing you to focus on growing your business while knowing that your legal matters are in capable hands.

Establishing a solid legal foundation is vital for the longevity and success of your business. By selecting the right legal structure, obtaining necessary registrations, and protecting your intellectual property, you ensure compliance and mitigate risks. Remember, the legal aspects of your business aren't just formalities – they're the framework that supports your entrepreneurial aspirations. As you delve into the legal landscape, approach each step with diligence and seek professional advice when needed, setting the stage for a thriving and legally sound business venture.

# CHAPTER 6:
# WRITING AND DEVELOPING A BUSINESS PLAN

A well-crafted business plan is more than a document; it's a roadmap that guides your business's journey, setting the course for growth, strategies, and success. This chapter delves into the essential components of a business plan, from outlining your mission and vision to defining your target audience and mapping out your strategies for long-term prosperity.

## Defining Your Mission and Vision

At the core of every successful business lies a clear and purpose-driven mission and vision. Your mission statement articulates why your business exists – its fundamental purpose and the impact it aims to make. It encapsulates the essence of your business's identity, serving as a compass that guides your decisions and actions.

Crafting a compelling mission statement involves introspection. What drives you to start this business? What problem are you solving, and what value are you bringing to the world? As you articulate your mission, envision the positive change you aspire to create – whether it's simplifying a complex process, enhancing people's lives, or revolutionizing an industry.

Equally vital is your vision statement – a vivid description of the future you're working toward. It's a glimpse of your ultimate destination, a motivational beacon that keeps you and your team aligned and motivated. Your vision encapsulates your aspirations, encapsulating the impact you hope to achieve, and the legacy you want to leave.

Crafting a compelling vision statement involves looking beyond the present and imagining the possibilities. What does success look like to you? What impact will your business have in five, ten, or twenty years? Your vision should be ambitious, inspiring, and a constant reminder of what you're working tirelessly to achieve.

## Understanding Your Target Audience

The success of your business hinges on your ability to understand and cater to your target audience's needs, desires, and pain points. Delving deep into your audience's demographics, behaviors, and preferences empowers you to tailor your offerings to their specific requirements.

Begin by creating detailed customer personas – fictional representations of your ideal customers. Consider factors like age, gender, income level, interests, and challenges. The more comprehensive your personas, the better you can tailor your products, services, and marketing strategies to resonate with your audience.

Market research is a powerful tool in understanding your target audience. Conduct surveys, analyze online behavior, and gather feedback to uncover insights. What problems are they trying to solve? What motivates their purchasing decisions? By immersing yourself in your audience's world, you gain invaluable insights that shape your business strategies.

Moreover, empathy plays a key role. Put yourself in your customers' shoes – understand their frustrations, aspirations, and emotions. When you empathize with your audience, you can create solutions that truly resonate. Remember, your business isn't just about transactions; it's about building relationships and solving problems for real people.

## Setting Clear Goals and Objectives

Goals and objectives form the backbone of your business's growth strategy. Setting clear, specific, and measurable goals is essential to ensure that your efforts are aligned and progress is quantifiable.

Start by defining your short-term and long-term goals. Short-term goals are the stepping stones that lead to your long-term vision. For instance, if your vision is to become a leading e-commerce platform, a short-term goal could be increasing website traffic by a certain percentage in the next six months.

To make your goals actionable, ensure they are SMART – Specific, Measurable, Achievable, Relevant, and Time-bound. Instead of saying "increase sales," set a goal like "achieve a 15% increase in sales by the end of the fiscal year." This specificity gives you a clear target to work towards.

Objectives break down your goals into actionable steps. They outline the strategies, tactics, and resources you'll employ to achieve your goals. Each objective should be aligned with your business's overall mission and vision, guiding your actions and decisions.

Constantly review and update your goals and objectives as your business evolves. As you accomplish one milestone, set new ones that propel you forward. This iterative process keeps your business dynamic and ensures that you're always progressing toward your ultimate vision.

## Crafting a Compelling Value Proposition

Your value proposition is the cornerstone of your business's identity – a succinct statement that communicates the unique benefits you offer to your customers. It's the answer to the question, "Why should someone choose your business over competitors?"

To craft a compelling value proposition, start by identifying the specific pain points your target audience faces. What problems are they looking to solve, and what challenges do they encounter? Your value proposition should position your offerings as solutions to these issues.

Focus on differentiation. What sets your business apart? It could be innovative technology, exceptional customer service, or a unique approach to a common problem. Highlight these differentiators in your value proposition to emphasize the value you bring that others don't.

Consider the emotional aspect. Beyond functional benefits, think about how your offerings make your customers feel. Does your product simplify their lives? Does your service alleviate stress? By tapping into the emotional resonance, you create a more profound connection with your audience.

Keep it concise and clear. Your value proposition should be easily understood and memorable. Avoid jargon and technical terms – use language that resonates with your audience and communicates benefits in a straightforward manner.

Regularly revisit and refine your value proposition. As your business evolves and customer needs shift, your value proposition may need adjustments. Continuously evaluate how well it aligns with your offerings and resonates with your target audience.

Remember, your value proposition is a promise you make to your customers. It's the foundation of your branding, marketing, and customer interactions. By crafting a compelling value proposition, you're not just selling a product or service – you're offering a solution that addresses your customers' needs and fulfills their aspirations.

## Developing a Marketing and Sales Strategy
A comprehensive plan for marketing and sales is an essential component of any sound business plan. Investigate a variety of channels for communicating with your target demographic, including but not limited to online marketing, social media, and more conventional forms of advertising. Gain the knowledge necessary to construct a sales funnel and create pricing strategies that are in line with the value proposition you offer.

## Analyzing the Competitive Landscape
It is essential to gain an understanding of your competitors in order to successfully carve out a niche in the market. Carry out a competitive analysis in order to determine the advantages, disadvantages, opportunities, and dangers posed by other companies operating within your industry. This knowledge helps you position your business in an effective manner and informs the strategies you use to differentiate your offering.

## Budgeting and Financial Projections
One of the most important aspects of a business plan is the inclusion of financial projections. Dive into the

fundamentals of budgeting, including the estimation of costs, the projection of revenues, and the prediction of profits. Your business's viability can be better understood through the use of financial projections, which can also assist in securing funding from investors or lenders.

## Implementing a Marketing and Promotional Plan

Your business plan should outline how you'll promote your products or services to your target audience. Develop a comprehensive marketing plan that includes strategies for online and offline promotion, PR efforts, events, and partnerships. A well-executed marketing plan can propel your business's visibility and growth.

## Creating an Actionable Timeline

A timeline outlines the milestones and deadlines your business aims to achieve. From product launches to expansion plans, a timeline keeps your goals on track and ensures accountability. Learn how to create a realistic timeline that guides your actions and helps you measure progress.

A business plan isn't just a formality – it's a dynamic tool that maps out your business's journey and guides your decisions. By defining your mission, understanding your audience, and setting clear goals, you create a strategic framework for success. As you write and develop your business plan, envision the future you want to create and let your plan serve as the compass that leads you there. With each component carefully crafted, you're setting the stage for a thriving and purposeful business venture.

# CHAPTER 7:
## MARKETING AND PROMOTION

Marketing and promotion are the engines that drive your business's growth, connecting your offerings with your target audience and creating a lasting impression. This chapter delves into the art of crafting an effective marketing strategy, utilizing various channels to reach your audience, and creating impactful promotional campaigns that resonate.

## Crafting Your Marketing Strategy

Your marketing strategy outlines how you'll position your business, communicate your value proposition, and engage with your audience. Explore the elements of a comprehensive strategy, including defining your unique selling points, identifying your marketing mix, and determining your brand voice.

## Harnessing the Power of Digital Marketing

In the digital age, online platforms offer unparalleled opportunities to connect with your audience. Dive into the world of digital marketing – from social media and content marketing to email campaigns and search engine optimization (SEO). Learn how to leverage these tools to boost your online presence.

## Creating Engaging Content

Content is the backbone of your online presence. Engaging content establishes your expertise, builds trust with your audience, and fosters a sense of community. This chapter guides you in crafting various types of content – from blog posts and videos to infographics – that resonate with your target audience.

### Building a User-Friendly Website

Your website is your virtual storefront, often the first interaction customers have with your business. Learn how to design a user-friendly website that not only showcases your offerings but also provides a seamless browsing experience. Elements like responsive design and clear navigation contribute to a positive user experience.

### Tapping into Social Media

Social media platforms are powerful tools for engagement and brand building. Understand the nuances of each platform – from Facebook and Instagram to LinkedIn and Twitter – and tailor your content to suit the preferences of your target audience. Social media allows you to connect, interact, and create a loyal following.

### Incorporating Traditional Marketing

While digital marketing is essential, traditional methods still have their place. Explore how tactics like print advertising, direct mail, and networking events can complement your online efforts. A balanced approach ensures that you reach a diverse audience and maximize your brand exposure.

### Measuring and Analyzing

Effective marketing is measurable. Dive into analytics tools that help you track key metrics, such as website traffic, conversion rates, and engagement levels. By analyzing these insights, you can refine your strategies, optimize your campaigns, and make informed decisions.

### Creating Impactful Promotional Campaigns

Promotional campaigns generate excitement and drive sales. Learn how to create campaigns that align with your brand identity and resonate with your audience. Whether it's a limited-time offer, a giveaway, or a special event, effective promotions can attract attention and boost customer engagement.

## Monitoring and Adjusting

The marketing landscape is dynamic, and what works today might not work tomorrow. Regularly monitor the performance of your marketing efforts and be ready to make adjustments based on the data. Flexibility and responsiveness are key to maintaining a competitive edge.

Marketing and promotion are the threads that weave your business into the fabric of your target audience's lives. By crafting a strategic marketing plan, utilizing digital and traditional channels, and creating engaging content, you establish a strong brand presence. As you embark on this journey, remember that marketing is not just about selling – it's about building relationships, nurturing trust, and delivering value to your customers. With each campaign, you have the opportunity to connect, inspire, and leave an indelible mark on your audience.

# CHAPTER 8:
# BUILDING A STRONG ONLINE PRESENCE

In the digital age, an online presence is more than a luxury – it's a necessity for connecting with your audience, establishing credibility, and driving business growth. This chapter delves into the strategies and tactics required to build a robust online presence that sets your business apart in the virtual world.

## Creating an Effective Website

Your website is your digital storefront, and it should captivate visitors from the moment they land on it. Learn how to design a visually appealing, user-friendly website that showcases your offerings, communicates your brand's personality, and guides visitors seamlessly toward their desired actions.

## Optimizing for Search Engines (SEO)

Search engine optimization (SEO) ensures that your website ranks well in search engine results, making it easier for potential customers to find you. Explore the fundamentals of SEO, including keyword research, on-page optimization, and link building. A strong SEO strategy enhances your online visibility and drives organic traffic.

## Harnessing the Power of Content Marketing

Content is the fuel that powers your online presence. Dive into content marketing – creating valuable, informative, and engaging content that resonates with your target audience. From blog posts and videos to ebooks and podcasts, content marketing positions you as an industry authority and draws visitors to your website.

## Engaging on Social Media Platforms

Social media platforms offer a direct line of communication with your audience. Understand the nuances of different platforms and create a consistent posting schedule that resonates with your followers. Engage in meaningful conversations, share valuable content, and build a loyal community around your brand.

## Leveraging Email Marketing

Email marketing remains a powerful tool for nurturing relationships with your audience. Learn how to build an email list, create compelling campaigns, and deliver content that adds value to your subscribers' lives. A well-executed email strategy keeps your audience informed and engaged.

## Exploring Paid Advertising

You can reach a specific demographic of people very quickly through paid advertising. Learn how to create successful advertising campaigns, whether you will be using pay-per-click (PPC) ads on search engines or advertising on social media platforms. These campaigns should generate clicks, conversions, and a healthy return on investment.

## Building Relationships through Influencer Marketing

Influencer marketing leverages the reach and credibility of individuals who have a strong online following. Explore how to identify relevant influencers, collaborate with them, and create authentic campaigns that introduce your brand to their audience.

## Monitoring Online Reputation

Your online reputation is a reflection of your brand's credibility and trustworthiness. Monitor online mentions, reviews, and feedback to ensure that your reputation remains positive. Address concerns promptly and engage with your audience in a transparent and authentic manner.

## Embracing Emerging Technologies

The digital landscape is ever-evolving, and emerging technologies offer new opportunities for engagement. From chatbots and virtual reality to interactive content, explore how these technologies can enhance user experiences and set your brand apart.

Building a strong online presence is an ongoing journey that requires a blend of strategy, creativity, and adaptability. By creating a captivating website, optimizing for search engines, and leveraging content marketing, you establish a solid foundation. As you engage with your audience on social media, nurture relationships through email marketing, and explore paid advertising, you're shaping a dynamic and influential online identity. In this digital realm, your online presence is more than a website or social media profiles – it's the bridge that connects you with your customers, enabling you to share your story, deliver value, and make a lasting impact.

# CONCLUSION: NAVIGATING YOUR ENTREPRENEURIAL JOURNEY

Congratulations, aspiring entrepreneur! You've embarked on a remarkable journey – one filled with challenges, triumphs, and the promise of turning your dreams into reality. As we conclude this guide on practical ways to start a successful business, let's reflect on the insights and strategies that have paved your path to success.

Starting a business is more than a venture; it's an embodiment of your passion, expertise, and determination. From the inception of your idea to the establishment of your brand identity, you've delved into critical aspects that lay the groundwork for a thriving enterprise.

You've learned that purpose drives every decision you make. Your business's mission and vision shape your trajectory, serving as a guiding light that keeps you focused on your goals. Embracing flexibility empowers you to navigate the ever-changing landscape of entrepreneurship, adapting to challenges while remaining aligned with your core values.

Guidance and counseling have illuminated your way forward, with mentors, associations, and resources offering insights that fuel your growth. Deciding on services provided and defining your target market ensures that your offerings resonate with your audience's needs.

Your legal structure and model establish the framework that safeguards your business's future, while a well-crafted business plan serves as your roadmap, guiding you through obstacles and opportunities alike. Marketing and promotion amplify your brand's voice, connecting you with your audience and fostering lasting relationships.

Building a strong online presence has positioned you in the digital realm, where your authenticity, content, and engagement have the power to inspire, influence, and captivate. Through every chapter of this guide, you've gained the tools and knowledge needed to turn your business idea into a reality.

As you venture forth, remember that entrepreneurship is a continuous learning experience. Challenges are opportunities in disguise, and each step you take – no matter how small – brings you closer to your vision. Embrace the journey with resilience, creativity, and an unwavering commitment to your purpose.

Your success story is waiting to be written. With each decision you make, every strategy you implement, and every connection you forge, you're shaping your legacy. May this guide serve as a steadfast companion on your entrepreneurial voyage, offering insights, guidance, and encouragement whenever you need it.

The world of business welcomes you with open arms. It's time to turn your aspirations into achievements, your dreams into reality. Embrace the adventure, navigate the challenges, and remember – you have the power to create a successful and impactful business that leaves a mark on the world. Best of luck on your journey!

# About the Authors

Aaron Robinson

Aaron Robinson was born on the West side of Chicago. He is the Chief Executive Officer of Robinson Publishing LLC that produces the national magazine, Consciousness Magazine, a leading publication, dedicated to inspiring, educating, and empowering readers by exposing them to topics related to personal growth, social justice, and community activism. He is also the host of the Aaron & Tocarra Show, presented by Consciousness Magazine.

With over 20 years of experience as a professional graphic designer, Mr. Robinson is an active art director for Allezom International Magazine and a professional graphic designer who has worked with various celebrities. Aside magazine publishing and graphics, Mr. Robinson is a prolific author of several books, including, *How to Self-Publish a Magazine, The Artwork of Aaron Robinson, Prestige Interviews I, Prestige Interviews II, Prestige Interviews III, Motivation and Inspirational Guide to Overcome Challenges and Obstacles in Life* and the co-author of *How to Start a Non-Profit Organization,* and *Teens' Basic Guide to Starting A Business.*

He has been published in numerous publications, featured on many local television shows, and selected to enter multiple art galleries and talent events, winning and earning numerous certificates and awards. Some of these awards include the NAACP Presidents Award, the Kankakee County Chamber Nonprofit of the Year Award, the Association of Business and Organization Best of 2019 and 2022 Award, and nominated for Soul Central Awards 2019/2020. Mr. Robinson has also been a guest speaker at universities, colleges, and high schools. He finds it fascinating to have many years of experience as a mentor and substitute teacher. His goal is to continue empowering youth and acting as a role model for our young generation.

Mr. Robinson also owns They Authentic Records, LLC, making a prominent name for himself in the music industry by presenting and bringing opportunities to his client artists. His music career began as a solo artist by the name of Comprehend. Mr. Robinson has released two albums, Epiphany Moments: The Book of Aaron and 16 Days Apart.

He has produced, written, and worked with industry icons such as international recording artist Tocarra, BenOne, Earl "LC", a former R&B group member of Public Announcement, Michael DeBarge and Keith Murray. Mr. Robinson has been advised by numerous industry greats, including Grammy Award-winning artist Gary Hines, Hezekiah Walker, Aaron "Hitman" Pittman, and the late Heavy D.

As an active community member and philanthropist, Mr. Robinson sits as Operational Manager on the Board of Directors for Still I Rise, a 501(c)3 organization geared towards poverty-stricken and disadvantaged youth. He is also an active board member of City of Kankakee CAB, Catalyst Advisory Committee, and the Neighborhood Master Plan initiative with his community's local politicians and business owners.

As an entrepreneur, Mr. Robinson continues to collaborate on various business ventures, striving to be diverse while making substantial artistic contributions as an innovator and philanthropist. He holds a Bachelor's degree in Arts and Science (Computer Graphic Design) from Columbia College Chicago and an Associate's degree in Fine Arts from Kankakee Community College.

Website: www.AaronRobinsonBooks.com

Tocarra Eldridge-Robinson

Tocarra Eldridge-Robinson is the President and founder of federally recognized 501(c)(3) tax-exempt non-profit organization, Still I Rise, which educates, inspires and empowers amongst youth and young adults to obtain self-sufficiency and confidence to ultimately make a positive difference in society. This innovative organization provides entrepreneurial and leadership development programming, along with invaluable mentoring to thousands of diverse youth and young adults via comprehensive and cohesive programs. Additionally, the organization feeds and clothes the homeless and those in need on a monthly basis. Still I Rise has been recognized frequently since its founding in 2014. Awards and honors include: 2021 Kankakee County Chamber of Commerce Nonprofit of the Year Award, 2021 NAACP President's Award, 2019 and 2022 Best of Kankakee Awards.

Robinson is extremely passionate about giving back to her community, as she also serves on various Boards and Committees. Her significant leadership skills are continuously displayed as she continues to be a successful and resourceful instrument to the business world. Driven by her passion for volunteerism and community activism, she works with a multitude of organizations and businesses, and also plays a significant role advocating for community change while working with Congressional and Political leaders, Scholars and Career experts. She frequently volunteers her time to several non-profit organizations, foundations, and community initiatives. Annually, Robinson volunteers for NBA Hall of Famer, Isiah Thomas', annual toy drive.

Robinson is currently pursuing a Doctorate degree in Organizational Leadership. She is a graduate of Roosevelt

University, where she earned her Master's degree in Public Administration, as she also interned for Congressman Danny K. Davis. Robinson earned her Bachelor of Arts degree in Criminal Justice from Governors State University. In her initial undergraduate studies, she double majored, earning both, an Associate of Arts degree in Criminal Justice and an Associate of Science degree in Law Enforcement.

She is the driving force behind a multitude of successful innovative businesses in her community. Robinson often consults individuals who desire to become established non-profit organization leaders, which led her to write and release her books How To Start a Non-profit Organization and Teens' Basic Guide to Starting A Business.

Outside of being a non-profit organization leader, Robinson is also a remarkable journalist whom has interviewed a massive amount of prominent individuals. While promoting her positive energy, she has worked alongside and interviewed industry greats including Danny Glover, Jeff Foxworthy, David and Tamela Mann and a host of more. Additionally, Robinson is a talk show host and professional recording artist.

Visit Still I Rise NPO website at www.Still-iRise.org

# ABOUT ROBINSON PUBLISHING LLC

Founded in 2018, Robinson Publishing, LLC is an in-house publishing company that publishes, distributes and sells paperback and eBooks. Our books contain valuable content and information that inspire and empower our readers. Some of the book types include Non-Fiction, Autobiographies, How-To Books, Guides, Poem Books and Children's Books. Robinson Publishing, LLC was derived from magazine publishing, where we successfully published and released national and international magazines since 2014. We expanded our brand to captivate a more diverse audience and avid book readers. We pride ourselves in quality and perfection. We have highly educated, experienced, aspiring and great authors and writers that are knowledgeable in their respected area of profession which makes us a unique company set apart from others.

Robinson Publishing, LLC
Contact: (312) 715-7884

www.ingramcontent.com/pod-product-compliance
Lightning Source LLC
Chambersburg PA
CBHW062236290526
45794CB00006B/2305